Audience

A Play

Václav Havel

Translated by
Vera Blackwell

Samuel French - London
New York - Toronto - Hollywood

AUDIENCE

Produced by BBC TV for the 1978/79 Play for Today
season with the following cast:

Vaněk   Michael Crawford
Head Maltster   Freddie Jones

Producer Innes Lloyd
Director Claude Watham

The action takes place in the Maltster's office
Time: the present

CHARACTERS

Ferdinand Vaněk
Head Maltster

Also by Václav Havel published by Samuel French Ltd

Private View

AUDIENCE

Maltster's office

There is a shabby desk littered with papers, empty bottles, a bottle opener and two glasses. Next to the desk is a crate with bottled beer and two old creaky wooden chairs

Maltster is sitting in his chair, his head resting on the desk, snoring loudly

There is a knock on the door

Maltster (*instantly waking up*) Come in.

The simple wooden door opens with a creak

Vaněk (*off*) Good morning—
Maltster Ah, Mr Vaněk! Come on in.

Vaněk enters and closes the door. We can hear his footsteps approaching on the plain wooden floor

Sit down.

The chair scrapes the floorboards and creaks. Vaněk, in padded work clothes and gumboots, timidly sits down oppposite Maltster

Have a lager.
Vaněk No thanks—
Maltster Go on! Lovely lager! You don't want all this lovely lager to go to waste? Eh?

He pulls a bottle out of the crate, opens it and pours two glasses

Pure gold! Here—

He pushes one glass across the desk towards Vaněk

Take it!
Vaněk Thank you—

Maltster gulps down his beer and smacks his lips

Maltster Ah! (*He pours the remains of the bottle into his glass. Pause*) Well, how's it going?

Vaněk All right, thank you—

Maltster It better be, eh?

Vaněk Mmnn—

Maltster (*after a pause*) What's it for you today, then? Handling casks?

Vaněk Just empties—

Maltster Handling empties is better than handling fulls, isn't it?

Vaněk Yes—

Maltster (*after a pause*) Who's handling fulls today, then?

Vaněk Sherkezy—

Maltster He clocked in, did he?

Vaněk Yes. A while ago—

Maltster Drunk?

Vaněk A bit—

Maltster (*after a pause*) Why don't you drink? Go on! Drink up!

Vaněk Thanks. I'm not much of a beer drinker—

Maltster Get off! Really? We'll see about that, don't worry! You'll get used to it in this place. We're all beer drinkers around here. Sort of local tradition, you know?

Vaněk I know—

Maltster (*after a pause*) Come on! Cheer up!

Vaněk I'm all right—

Maltster (*after a pause*) Well, how's everything?

Vaněk What do you mean?

Maltster I mean, on the whole—

Vaněk Not too bad, thank you—

Maltster (*after a pause*) How do you like it here, then?

Vaněk I like it—

Maltster Could be worse, eh?

Vaněk Yes—

Maltster opens another bottle and pours himself a glass

Maltster One gets used to anything, right?

Vaněk Yes—

Maltster (*after a pause*) Finish your glass!

Vaněk drinks up and Maltster pours him some more

Vaněk No more, please—

Maltster You must be joking. Haven't even started, have you? (*Pause*) How about the lads, then? Get on with them all right?

Vaněk Quite all right, thanks—

Maltster Let me give you a piece of advice. You don't want to get too matey with anybody around here! I trust nobody in this place! People are real bastards, you know! Real bastards! You can take it from me! Just mind your job, and better stay away from the other blokes! No good mucking about eh? Specially in your position.

Vaněk I know what you mean—

Maltster (*after a pause*) Well, what sort of stuff did you write, if you don't mind my asking?

Vaněk Plays—

Maltster Plays? You mean they were put on in some theatre?

Vaněk Yes—

Maltster Mmnn. Well, fancy that! Plays for the theatre, eh? Listen, you ought to write something about our brewery! About Bures, for example. You know him?

Vaněk Yes—

Maltster He's a right character, what?

Vaněk Yes—

Maltster (*after a pause*) Come on! Cheer up!

Vaněk I'm all right—

Maltster (*after a pause*) Anyway, I bet it never even crossed your mind, eh?

Vaněk What's never crossed my mind?

Maltster Well, that one day you'll be humping casks in a brewery!

Vaněk Mmnn—

Maltster Some paradox, eh?

Vaněk Mmnn—

Maltster I'll say that! (*Pause*) It's handling empties for you today, you said.

Vaněk Yes—

Maltster But yesterday you handled fulls. Saw you with my own eyes.

Vaněk Sherkezy wasn't here yesterday—

Maltster You're all right, you know! (*Pause*) Never had a writer here before. And, mind you, we've had some odd customers round here! Well, take this Bures, for example. You know what he was? A gravedigger! That's where he learned to knock it

back, and that's why he landed in here. The stories he can tell!
Marvellous!

Vaněk I know—

Maltster What were your plays about, then?

Vaněk About white-collar workers, mostly—

Maltster Get away! White-collar workers? Really? Mmnn—
(*Pause*) Had your morning break yet?

Vaněk Not yet—

Maltster You can take it later. Just tell them at the gate you were
here with the Head Maltster.

Vaněk Thank you—

Maltster Oh, come on! What do you want to go on thanking me
for? (*Pause*) Anyway, I respect you, you know.

Vaněk Me? What for?

Maltster Must be pretty rough on you, not being accustomed, see?
After all, just sitting around the house all your life, nice and
warm, sleeping until all hours in the morning, and—bingo—
now this! No, really, I mean it! I respect that—(*Pause*) Excuse
me—won't be a minute—(*He gets up, the chair creaks*)

Maltster exits, his footsteps on the floorboards receding

A door is opened, off

Vaněk quickly pours the rest of his beer into Maltster's glass

Vaněk There! He won't know the difference.

*A lavatory is flushed, off, then the door is closed and footsteps on the
floorboards approach*

Maltster enters

Maltster (*with a sigh of relief*) Ah! That's better. (*He sits down.
The chair creaks*) Bet you got to know all kinds of actresses
when you used to write for the theatre.

Vaněk Naturally—

Maltster Like Bohdalova, for instance?

Vaněk Yes—

Maltster You know her? In person?

Vaněk Yes—

Maltster Well, suppose you ask her down here for a pint or two, eh?—We could take Bures along with us—Could be lots of fun, eh? What do you say?

Vaněk Mmnn—

Pause. Maltster drains his glass

Maltster Come on! Cheer up!

Vaněk I'm all right—

Maltster opens another bottle and pours himself and Vaněk a glass. Pause

Maltster That youngster from the fermenting room—know who I mean?

Vaněk Mlynarik?

Maltster You want to watch it when he's around! (*Pause*) And how about this pop singer, Karel Gott? Happen to be acquainted with him, too?

Vaněk Yes, I know him—

Maltster (*after a pause*) Pity you weren't here 'bout five years ago! Was a fabulous mob in here then! You won't find anything like that around here today! The booze-ups we had here in those days! Used to get together in the maltings—myself, another bloke, a Kaja Maranek, isn't here any more, Honza Peterka, the girls over from bottling—many times we carried right on until the small hours. And, mind you, all the work got done, regardless! You go and ask Honza Peterka! He'll tell you all about it.

Vaněk He's told me about it already—

Maltster (*after a pause*) How much did you make, then? From those plays, you know?

Vaněk It varied—

Maltster Round about five grand, eh?

Vaněk It depends how often they're performed and by how many theatres. There are times one gets plenty of money, and other times one gets nothing at all—

Maltster Like nothing a whole month?

Vaněk Could be several months—

Maltster So there's a catch in your game too, eh? Same as in everything else!

Vaněk Yes—

Maltster Anyway, some paradox, what?

Vaněk Mmnn—

Maltster I'll say that! (*Pause*) Come on! You're not drinking!

Vaněk But I am—(*He drinks with effort*)

Maltster How about the other half, then?

Maltster opens another bottle and pours Vaněk and himself a glass

Vaněk No more!

Maltster Oh, get on! (*Pause*) Listen, let me tell you something. Just between you and me. If there was somebody else here in my place, you can lay odds you wouldn't be working with us now!

Vaněk Was there trouble?

Maltster You bet!

Vaněk I'm very grateful to you—

Maltster Mind you, I don't want to sort of—you know—but when I see I can do a chap a good turn—well, I say to myself, why not. Eh? That's the sort of man I am—even today! The way I see it, people got to help each other out. This time I help you, next time you help me, right?

Vaněk Yes—

Maltster (*after a pause*) Had your morning break yet?

Vaněk Not yet—

Maltster You can take it later. Just tell them at the gate you were here with the Head Maltster.

Vaněk Thank you—

Maltster Oh, come on! What do you want to go on thanking me for? (*Pause*) Mind you, nobody wants to get his fingers burnt these days!

Vaněk I know—

Maltster (*after a pause*) Main thing, we all got to stick together, as the saying goes.

Vaněk Yes—

Maltster You know, I don't know what you think, but I always say, a good team is the basis of everything.

Vaněk I agree with you—

Maltster Why don't you drink? I expect you'd prefer some of your fancy wine, eh?

Vaněk Mmnn—

Maltster You'll get used to beer in this place. We're all beer drinkers around here. Sort of local tradition, you know?

Vaněk I know—
Maltster (*after a pause*) Are you married?
Vaněk Yes—
Maltster Any children?
Vaněk None—
Maltster (*after a pause*) Anyway, I respect you.
Vaněk Now, look here—
Maltster I mean it! Must be pretty rough on you, not being accustomed, see? (*Pause*) Excuse me—won't be a minute—(*The chair creaks as he gets up*)

Maltster exits

The door is opened, off, his footsteps recede

Vaněk quickly pours the rest of his beer into Maltster's glass

Vaněk There! He won't know the difference.

A lavatory is flushed, off, the door is shut and footsteps approach

Maltster enters

Maltster (*with a sigh of relief*) Ah! That's better. (*He sits down. The chair creaks*) How old is she, then?
Vaněk Who?
Maltster Bohdalova, of course!
Vaněk About forty-three, I think—
Maltster Get away! Sure doesn't look it! (*Pause*) Listen, I mean it! Things're going to be all right! We just got to help each other out, that's all. We got to stick together, as the saying goes. Well, the point is, as I always say, a good team is the basis of everything! (*He opens another bottle and pours himself a glass*) Pity you weren't here 'bout five years ago! Was a fabulous mob in here then! You won't find anything like that round here today. Today I trust nobody in this place! (*Pause*) Tell me, who's this chap, Kohout?
Vaněk What do you mean?
Maltster They say a Kohout came to see you.
Vaněk Oh! Well, he's one of my former colleagues—

Maltster Another writer?

Vaněk Yes. What about it?

Maltster Never mind. (*Pause*) Now don't go around thinking I got no troubles of my own, Vaněk!

Vaněk Well, I—but, after all, you're the Head Maltster in this brewery—

Maltster In this hole, you mean! Why do you think I got stuck in this hole, eh? But I don't think this'll interest you—

Vaněk Oh, but it does—

Maltster You realize what job I was offered? What I was supposed to be?

Vaněk No. What?

Maltster The Head Maltster in the Pardubice brewery!

Vaněk Really?

Maltster That's right! And look at me now! Some paradox, eh?

Vaněk But why didn't you take the job over there?

Maltster Oh, forget it! (*Pause*) Are you married?

Vaněk Yes—

Maltster Any children?

Vaněk None—

Maltster (*after a pause*) Look it's none of my business, but you better tell this Holub not to come and see you again.

Vaněk You mean my colleague Kohout—

Maltster What did I say?

Vaněk Holub—

Maltster Look, it's none of my business. I wouldn't know that bloke from another, I've no idea what sort of chap he is. I'm only telling you in your own best interests.

Vaněk Well, I'm sorry, but I—

Maltster Look, mate, you sip it like it was brandy!

Vaněk But I told you, I'm not much of a beer drinker—

Maltster Kaw! Get off!

Vaněk I mean it—

Maltster I know. You don't want to drink with me. I'm not good enough for you, eh?

Vaněk But really, I assure you—

Maltster I realize I'm no pop star, like your Karel Gott! I'm just a common brewery mug, that's all!

Vaněk But you're a professional in your line of work, the way Gott is one in his. Why didn't you take the job in Pardubice?

Maltster Oh, forget it!

He opens another bottle and pours a glass for himself. Pause

Things're going to be all right, Vaněk! Don't you worry, I'm
going to look after you! You're a mild, hard-working sort of
bloke, you clock in regular every day, no griping about everything like all the others, no grumbling about your pay-packet,
eh? And bearing in mind the shortage of labour, well—

Vaněk I'm very grateful to you—

Maltster Besides, you're a decent chap, I can tell, I got a nose for
this sort of thing. Can smell a villain a mile away! Take this
Mlynarik from the fermenting room—you know who I mean?

Vaněk Yes—

Maltster I sized him up the moment he walked in! You want to
watch him!

Vaněk (*after a pause*) Why didn't you take the job in Pardubice?

Maltster Oh, forget it! (*Pause*) Thing is, you can count on me,
Vaněk. I'm not going to let you down!

Vaněk Thank you—

Maltster All I want, I want to be sure that I can count on you!
That you're not going to pull a fast one on me! That I can rely
on you, that's all.

Vaněk I think you'll be pleased with my work—

Maltster There was no need for me to tell you. As a matter of fact,
I wasn't even supposed to tell you. Anybody else in my place—

Vaněk I'm sorry, but what was it you weren't supposed to tell me?

Maltster Well, about this chap, Holub—

Vaněk You mean Kohout—

Maltster Look here, I haven't the faintest what sort of a bloke he
is, and it's none of my business. Couldn't care less about him,
can cop it, as far as I'm concerned. What I care about is you,
see? The way things are, you aren't too badly off in here. You
just handle a few empties, nobody bothers you, eh? Your pal,
Kohout, isn't going to give you a job, dammit, if I can't keep
you on in here, is he? Eh? Is he?

Vaněk Well—hardly—

Maltster There you are! Come on, mate, grow up!

Vaněk (*after a pause*) I'm sorry—er—

Maltster What is it?

Vaněk Forgive me, but I—

Maltster What?

Vaněk I mean, surely I can—er—

Maltster You can what?

Vaněk Forgive me, but—I mean, surely I can see anybody I like—

Maltster That's exactly what I said! Didn't I say that? Go on, see anybody you like! That's your inviolable right! Nobody can muck about with that! You don't want anybody to take that away from you! For God's sake! You're a man, not a toe-rag! That's basic!

Vaněk Well, that's it then, isn't it?

Maltster I'm sure your pal, Kohout, will understand that from now on you're going to see anybody you like! Eh?

He opens another bottle and pours a glass for himself. Pause

Vaněk I'm sorry—er—

Maltster What is it?

Vaněk I've got to go now—

Maltster Where do you want to go?

Vaněk They'll be looking for me in the cellar—

Maltster Eh, stuff them! They got Sherkezy, haven't they? You just stay where you are and drink! (*Pause*) Listen, you don't care to know why I didn't take that job in Pardubice?

Vaněk Of course I do—

Maltster You mean it?

Vaněk I do. Why didn't you take that job?

Maltster You know what they did to me? They accused me I went partners with a publican and said we nicked five thousand crates of strong beer that was lying here surplus! Makes you puke, eh? Mind you, wasn't anything like that! Only this creep, this Mlynarik from the fermenting room—you know who I mean?

Vaněk Yes—

Maltster Just so you'd realize the sort of people we've got around here! I trust nobody in this place! People are real bastards, you know! Real bastards! You can take it from me! Just mind your job, and better stay away from the other blokes. No good mucking about, eh? Specially in your position.

Vaněk I know what you mean—

Maltster (*after a pause*) Had your morning break yet?

Vaněk Not yet—

Maltster You can take it later. Just tell them at the gate you were here, with the Head Maltster.

Vaněk Thank you—

Maltster Oh, get off! What do you want to go on thanking me for? (*Pause*) Excuse me—won't be a minute—

Maltster gets up and exits

The sequence of Vaněk's beer switch, the flushing of the lavatory and Maltster's re-entry take place exactly as before

Maltster Ah! That's better. (*He sits down, the chair creaks*) When do you want to bring her then?

Vaněk Whom?

Maltster Bohdalova, who else?

Vaněk Well, I'll see what can be done next time we happen to meet—

Maltster Suppose you ask her for Saturday.

Vaněk This coming Saturday?

Maltster Why not?

Vaněk Well, I—I've no idea if she's free—

Maltster Come on! She'll make herself free for you! Eh?

Vaněk But you see—actresses are very busy people—they're committed long in advance. They can't make any changes, just like that—

Maltster Sure, if you think we're not good enough for her in here, forget it. No need for you to bother.

Vaněk That's not what I meant—

Maltster Look, I'm not going to twist your arm. All I was thinking, I thought we might have a bit of fun, that's all.

Vaněk Mmnn—

Maltster (*after a pause*) Come on! Cheer up!

Vaněk I'm all right—

Maltster (*after a pause*) Listen Ferdinand—your name is Ferdinand isn't it?

Vaněk Yes—

Maltster Listen, Ferdinand, I want to have a word with you.

Vaněk I know—

Maltster (*after a pause*) Why don't you drink?

Vaněk But I told you, I'm afraid I don't like beer—

Maltster Everybody likes beer in this place.

Vaněk I know—

Maltster (*after a pause*) Listen, Ferdinand—you don't mind my calling you that, do you?

Vaněk No—Not at all—

Maltster What do you say about being the Stock Checker in our fulls store? Not bad, eh? After all, you're what you might call an intellectual, also you're honest—well? How about it? You don't want to go on handling casks with the gypsies! You'll have a little office all to yourself, you'll keep warm—lock up during the lunch hour—make out you're doing a bit of clearing up—and carry on thinking up some gags for those plays of yours in peace and quiet! You might even have a little shut-eye in there, if you like. Well, what do you say?

Vaněk You think there might be a chance?

Maltster There's always a chance!

Vaněk Of course, I'm in no position to pick and choose, but if it is at all possible—naturally, I'd be delighted! I'm fairly tidy, I think—I can type—I know a few languages—Well, I can't deny it is pretty cold down in that cellar—particularly when one isn't accustomed.

Maltster Exactly. Know anything about book-keeping?

Vaněk I'm sure I can learn—I had four terms of economics—

Maltster You did? And you know about book-keeping?

Vaněk I'm sure I can learn—

Maltster You'll keep warm—lock up during the lunch hour—You don't want to go on handling casks with the gypsies!

Vaněk Well, if there really was a chance—

Maltster (*after a pause*) No, no, Vaněk! When there's a villain around, I can smell him a mile away! You're an honest bloke, same here, so I don't see why the two of us couldn't team up! Eh? What do you say?

Vaněk Yes—of course—

Maltster Is it a deal, then?

Vaněk Certainly—

Maltster If you don't like it, just say so! Perhaps you mind going partners with me—perhaps you've some objections against me—perhaps you've some other plans—

Vaněk But I've no objections against you! On the contrary—you've done so much for me—I'm very grateful to you—particularly if it should come out about that little office in the fulls store. I'll do what I can. I think you'll be pleased with my work.

Maltster opens another bottle and pours a glass for Vaněk and himself

Maltster Shall we drink to it?

Vaněk Yes—

They both drink

Maltster Go on! Bottoms up!

Vaněk finishes his glass, with difficulty. Maltster instantly pours him another. Pause

Maltster Come on! Cheer up!

Vaněk I'm all right—

Maltster (*after a pause*) Listen, Ferdinand.

Vaněk Yes?

Maltster We're mates, eh?

Vaněk Yes—

Maltster You're not saying it just to please me?

Vaněk No—

Maltster You trust me, then?

Vaněk But of course I trust you—

Maltster Wait a minute! Now, be honest, eh? You trust me?

Vaněk I trust you—

Maltster Well then, look here, mate—I'm going to tell you something. But this is strictly between you and me, right?

Vaněk Right!

Maltster Sure?

Vaněk Sure!

Maltster Well, look here, mate—(*he lowers his voice*)—they keep coming here asking questions about you—

Vaněk Who?

Maltster *They*, who else!

Vaněk Really?

Maltster That's right!

Vaněk Is it your impression that my job here in the brewery is somehow—in jeopardy? (*Pause*) Are they leaning on you to give me the sack? (*Pause*) Or do they hold it against you that you hired me? Do they?

Maltster (*after a pause*) Well, look here, mate—I'm going to tell
  you something. But it's strictly between you and me, right?
Vaněk Right!
Maltster Sure?
Vaněk Sure!
Maltster Well, look here, mate—if there was somebody else here
  in my place, you can lay odds you wouldn't be working with us
  now! Get the drift?
Vaněk Yes, of course—I'm very grateful to you—
Maltster I'm not telling you so you'll thank me.
Vaněk I know that—
Maltster It's just so you'll realize what the score is.
Vaněk Thank you—
Maltster (*after a pause*) Excuse me—won't be a minute—

  He gets up with some difficulty and staggers as he exits

  *The sequence of Vaněk's beer switch, the flushing of the lavatory and
  Maltster's re-entry take place exactly as before*

Maltster Ah! That's better. (*He sits down. The chair creaks*) Did
  you have it off with her then?
Vaněk With whom?
Maltster With Bohdalova, who else?
Vaněk Me? No—
Maltster Get on!
Vaněk I didn't—
Maltster Well! Then as far as I'm concerned, you're a washout!
Vaněk (*after a pause*) I'm sorry—er—
Maltster What is it?
Vaněk I've got to go now—
Maltster Where do you want to go?
Vaněk They'll be looking for me in the cellar—
Maltster Eh, stuff them! They've got Sherkezy, haven't they? You
  just stay where you are and drink! (*Pause*) Listen, Ferdinand—
  your name is Ferdinand, isn't it?
Vaněk Yes—
Maltster Listen, Ferdinand—You don't mind my calling you
  Ferdinand, do you?
Vaněk Not at all—

Maltster Now, wait a minute! Let's be quite sure about that! You
  could take offence, for all I know!
Vaněk Why should I take offence?
Maltster One never knows where one stands with you—you keep
  your mouth shut—God knows what you're thinking! All you
  say, you say, "yes", "thank you", "I'm sorry"—
Vaněk That's the way I was brought up—
Maltster Whereas I'm just a mug from a brewery! Eh? Nobody
  brought me up, eh? That's what you mean, what? Don't try and
  tell me it's not what you mean!
Vaněk It isn't what I mean—
Maltster Now, come on, level with me! So I know where I stand!
Vaněk But I've never thought anything unkind about you, I
  assure you, never! On the contrary—
Maltster So we're mates, right?
Vaněk Yes—
Maltster You trust me, then?
Vaněk I trust you—
Maltster Well now, look here, mate. I happen to know one of the
  blokes that keep asking me questions about you—used to go to
  school together—old friend of mine, see? A Tonda Masek—not
  a bad bloke, least he takes my side—
Vaněk Good for you—
Maltster Not that he's got all that much influence. But he helped
  me out a couple of times already with this and that. There's no
  telling when one may be needing his assistance again. Besides, as
  I say, he's not a bad sort—so, you see. Well, the long and the
  short of it is—I just couldn't let him down! See what I mean?
Vaněk I see—
Maltster (*after a pause*) What do you look at me like that for?
Vaněk I'm not looking—
Maltster Go on, say what you're thinking! Come on, then, let's
  have it!
Vaněk I'm not thinking anything—
Maltster Get off! I know what you're thinking! Only it never
  crossed your mind that if I don't go along with them, they'll find
  somebody else! And that's bound to be much worse for you,
  because you can lay odds it's not going to be a fair bloke like
  myself! I happen to be straight, see, not like all the others!
  That's the sort of man I am—even today! And mind you, that's

where you were damned lucky! People are real bastards, you know. Real bastards! You mean you could find another nit around here who's going to lay his cards on the table like this? Eh? The way you're thinking it's like you've never grown up! Where do you think you're living, eh?

Vaněk I do appreciate your sincerity—

Maltster You realize the risks I'm taking being fair with you in this way? Supposing you pull a fast one on me, what then? Suppose you go and grass, eh? I'm putting myself at your mercy, as a matter of fact!

Vaněk I'm not going to tell anybody—

Maltster You're going to write about it, then! You're going to shove it into one of your plays—and they'll have me in the nick—and I'll be finished!

Vaněk I assure you, I won't say a word—

Maltster Sure?

Vaněk Sure—

Maltster opens another bottle and pours a glass for himself. Pause

Vaněk I'm sorry—er—

Maltster Mmnn?

Vaněk Suppose it works out—I mean, regarding that little office in the fulls store—what about old Sustr? Where would he go?

Maltster What about him? (*Pause*) Anyway, some paradox eh?

Vaněk Mmnn—

Maltster I'll say that!

Vaněk (*after a pause*) I'm sorry—er—

Maltster Mmnn?

Vaněk The little office in the fulls store—you think they'll give the permission? After all, they're bound to know I'd be more comfortable there, I'd be warm—

Maltster The hell they know! (*Pause*) Are you married?

Vaněk Yes—

Maltster Any children?

Vaněk None—

Maltster I got three. Just for your information.

Vaněk (*after a pause*) Perhaps you might argue that I'd be more isolated in there—

Maltster Listen, Ferdinand—

Vaněk After all, they do want me to stay away from the other men, don't they?

Maltster Listen, Ferdinand—

Vaněk It might be an argument, mightn't it?

Maltster Listen, Ferdinand—

Vaněk Yes?

Maltster You play darts?

Vaněk No—

Maltster I do. Used to have a cracking team in here once—every Thursday, you know—And what do you think happened? Had to give it up, too—on account of a certain Lojza Hlavaty—

Vaněk Mmnn—

Maltster Just so you'd realize it's not easy for any of us . . . (*Pause*) Listen, Ferdinand—

Vaněk Yes?

Maltster Ever met my Missis?

Vaněk No—

Maltster (*after a pause*) Listen, Ferdinand—

Vaněk Yes?

Maltster Screw it all! The lot!

Vaněk I know what you mean—

Maltster Like hell you know! You? You're all right, mate! You just carry on writing your plays, humping your casks—and the rest can stuff it! What more do you want? They're afraid of you, you know that?

Vaněk Oh, come on—

Maltster That's a fact! But what about me? Nobody gives a damn about me! Nobody sends any reports upstairs about me! They can kick me around any way they like! They have me cornered! They can crush me like a worm any time they want. Like a worm! But you? You're all right! (*Pause*) Listen, Ferdinand—

Vaněk Yes?

Maltster About the Bohdalova—you'll bring her here, won't you? Won't you? You're not going just to forget it! Eh? Is that a promise?

Vaněk I assure you—I'll call her today and arrange it with her—

Maltster You think she'll come?

Vaněk I'll do my best—

Maltster But you two are friends, right?

Vaněk Well, yes—

Maltster Now, wait a minute! You said you're friends!

Vaněk We are.

Maltster Where's the snag, then? (*Pause*) Damn it, you can be friends with anybody you like!

Vaněk Of course—

Maltster That's your inviolable right, dammit!

Vaněk Certainly—

Maltster That's basic, dammit, isn't it? (*Pause*) Anyway, nobody needs to know how she got here. It'll be just a run-of-the-mill get-together with the workers, eh? Nothing wrong about that, what?

Vaněk I don't think so—

Maltster You'll bring her, then?

Vaněk I'll do my best—I'll call her today—we're friends—nothing wrong with that—

Maltster (*after a pause*) Listen, Ferdinand—

Vaněk Yes?

Maltster If you only knew how pissed off I'm about everything!

Vaněk I know—

Maltster Like hell you know! You say to yourself, look at that nit, just let him talk—

Vaněk I'm not saying to myself anything of the sort—

Maltster Go on, then! Drink up!

Vaněk But I am drinking—

Maltster Had your morning break?

Vaněk Not yet—

Maltster Stuff the break!

Vaněk I don't care—

Maltster Perhaps I'm a nit, but you can't say I'm not fair!

Vaněk Of course you are—

Maltster I want to have a word with you.

Vaněk I know—

Maltster People are real bastards! Real bastards! Go on! Drink up!

Vaněk I am drinking—

Maltster Had your break?

Vaněk Not yet—

Maltster You? You're all right!

Vaněk I'm very grateful to you—

Maltster Eh, screw it all!

He opens another bottle and pours himself another glass. Pause

   Listen—
Vaněk Yes?
Maltster You don't mind my being familiar?
Vaněk No—
Maltster If you happen to mind, just go on and say so!
Vaněk I don't mind—
Maltster Well, that's something, isn't it? Least you don't mind!
Vaněk On the contrary, I'm very glad we've got better
   acquainted—
Maltster "I'm glad we've got better acquainted," "I appreciate
   your sincerity"—Tell me, why do you talk like—like—
Vaněk Like a book?
Maltster That's right.
Vaněk If it irritates you, I'll—
Maltster Nothing irritates me—I appreciate we got acquainted—
   shit!
Vaněk Sorry?
Maltster Shit!
Vaněk (*after a pause*) I'm sorry—er—
Maltster What is it?
Vaněk I've got to go now—
Maltster Where do you want to go?
Vaněk They'll be looking for me in the cellar—
Maltster Eh, stuff them! They've got Sherkezy haven't they? You
   just stay where you are and drink!
Vaněk Really—they'll be angry with me—
Maltster I see! I can take a hint! I'm boring you, eh? I know what
   you mean! Booze-ups with singer Gott and actress Bohdalova,
   that's another cup of tea altogether, what?
Vaněk I enjoy being here with you, really! Only, I'm afraid there
   might be some remarks—there's no point, is there—particularly
   now when there's this chance of a job in the fulls store—
Maltster You mean you enjoy being here with me? Really?
Vaněk I do—
Maltster You don't say that just to please me?
Vaněk No—

Maltster opens another bottle and pours a glass for himself. Pause

Maltster Ferdinand—

Vaněk Yes?

Maltster You know what's the worst thing about all this?

Vaněk What?

Maltster That I'm at my wit's end what I'm supposed to tell them week in, week out! What do I know about you? Not much. We don't really ever get together. And the few bits of gossip that come my way are no bloody good. That you take extra breaks in the laboratory—somebody saw you in town couple of times with Maruska from bottling—some blokes from maintenance helped to fix your heating at home—so what? See what I mean? What am I supposed to keep on telling them? You tell me! Well, what?

Vaněk I can hardly be of any help to you there—I'm sorry—

Maltster Sure you can! That is, if you want—

Vaněk Me? What do you mean?

Maltster You're what you'd call an intellectual, eh? You know the political set-up, right? You know how to write, don't you? Well then, who knows better than yourself the sort of things they want to know! Eh?

Vaněk I'm sorry, but surely that seems a bit—

Maltster Look, you'll have plenty of time in that little office in the fulls store. Can't be all that much trouble for a bloke like yourself to put it down on paper for me once a week, eh? I'm worth that much to you, ain't I? I'm going to look after you! You'll be in clover in there! You'll be able to get as much beer for yourself as you like in there! It'll be child's play for you! You're a writer, dammit! This Tonda Masek happens to be a decent bloke, you know, and he happens to be in need of a bit of assistance, see what I mean? So we can't let him down! Right? Didn't we just promise one another we're going to help one another? That the two of us are going to team-up? Eh? Didn't we just drink to it? Well, go on—did we drink to it, or didn't we?

Vaněk Well yes, but surely—

Maltster The whole thing now depends on you, Ferdinand. If you help us out, things are going to be all right. You help me, I help him, he helps me, I help you—and nobody's going to be the loser. We don't want to mess up our lives, do we? (*Pause*) Well, what do you look at me like that for?

Vaněk I'm not looking—

Maltster (*after a pause*) You'll have direct influence on what they know about you. That's nothing to be sneered at, is it?

Vaněk I know—

Maltster (*after a pause*) You'll be all right in that little office in the fulls store, eh? It's warm in there—you'll have plenty of time, eh?

Vaněk Sounds marvellous—

Maltster (*after a pause*) Well, where's the snag, then?

Vaněk (*after a pause*) I'm sorry—er—

Maltster What is it?

Vaněk I'm really very grateful to you for all you've done for me. I do appreciate it, because I know myself only too well how rare this sort of stand happens to be today. You pulled the thorn out of my flesh, so to speak. Honestly, I've no idea what I'd have done without your help. That job in the fulls store would be an enormous relief to me, perhaps greater than you think. Only— the thing is—please forgive me—but really I can't very well inform on myself—

Maltster What do you mean, inform? Who says anything about informing?

Vaněk I'm not concerned about myself. It couldn't do me any harm. But it's a matter of principle, isn't it? As a matter of principle I cannot actually participate in—

Maltster In what? Well, go on! What is it you cannot participate in?

Vaněk In a practice with which I do not agree!

Maltster (*after a short, tense pause*) Mmnn. So you can't! You "actually cannot" do it! That's marvellous! Now you've shown your true colours! Now we know who you really are! (*He gets up and starts walking about in great agitation*) What about me, then, eh? You just leave me holding the baby, eh? You don't give a damn about me! It's all right with you, if I'm a bastard, if I wade in the muck-heap! Why not? I'm just a common brewery mug! But the gentleman, that's another matter! No Sir, the gentleman "cannot participate"! It's all right if I get filthy—so long as the gentleman stays clean! The gentleman cares about a principle! But what about the rest of us, eh? He couldn't care less! So long as he looks pretty! A principle is more important to him than a human being! You're all the same! The lot of you!

Vaněk Who?

Maltster Who? You! Intellectuals! Gentlemen! Just mumbo-
jumbo, la-di-da words, that's all you know! And why not? You
can afford it! Nothing's ever going to happen to you! Everybody's interested in you! You know all the angles! You know
how to stick up for yourselves! You're up even when you're
down! But an ordinary bloke's just got to carry on! And what's
the good of all his drudgery? Shit! That's what! There's nobody
will speak out for him! Nobody gives a damn about him,
everybody can sweep the floor with him, everybody can order
him around, he's got nothing out of life, and in the end the
gentleman comes and tells him he got no principles! You
wouldn't mind taking a cushy job in the fulls store from me, eh?
But when it comes to taking with it also a bit of muck I got to
wade in every day, no Sir! No, that's too much for the gent!
You're all very clever, the lot of you! You know the whole
bloody set-up, and you know damned well how to look after
yourselves! Principles! Principles! Sure you hang on to your
flipping principles! Why not? You know damned well how to
cash in on them, you know there's always a market for them,
you know bloody well how to sell them at a profit! Thing is, you
live on your flipping principles! But what about me? All I can
expect is a kick in the pants if I so much as mention a principle!
You always got a chance, but what chance have I got? Nobody's
ever going to look after me, nobody's afraid of me, nobody's
going to write about me, nobody's going to help me, nobody
takes an interest in me! I'm only good enough to be the manure
on which your flaming principles can grow! Good enough to
find warm offices for the likes of you in which you can carry on
being heroes! And what do I get for all my trouble? Eh? Bloody
ridicule! That's what! One of these days you're going to go back
to your actresses, you're going to show off to them about the
way you handled casks in the brewery, and you'll be a hero! But
what about me? What do you think I got to go back to? Who's
going to take any notice of me? Who's ever going to appreciate
the things I've done? What have I got out of life? What's in store
for me? Eh? What future have I got? (*He slumps, depressed, into
his chair, which creaks. He rests his head on the desk and begins to
sob loudly. After a while he calms down, looks up at Vaněk and
softly asks*) Ferdinand?
Vaněk Mmnn—

Maltster Are we mates?

Vaněk We are—

Maltster Please go and fetch her—bring her here right now—I beg
you. (*Pause*) Tell her, "Listen, love, I got a mate—just a brewery
mug, you know—but he's an honest bloke!" (*Pause*) I'm going
to fight and get that job in the fulls store for you—I'm not going
to ask you for any reports—just do this one thing for me—that's
the only thing I want you to do—please! (*Pause*) You're going
to do it for me, aren't you? You'll do it, won't you? Just one
evening, that's all—I'll be all right then—things are going to be
different after that—then I'll know that I didn't live for
nothing—that my bloody life wasn't so damned bloody
awful!—You'll bring her, won't you? (*Pause. Then he begins to
shout in despair*) If you don't bring her—I—I don't know—I
think I'll—I'll—I'll—I don't know—(*He starts to cry softly and
again rests his head on his desk. After a while his sobbing slowly
changes into loud snoring*)

*Vaněk gently gets up and walks over to the door. At the door he halts
and turns*

Vaněk Come on! Cheer up!

Vaněk exits and the door closes with a creak

*After a short pause the lavatory is flushed in the distance, then there
is a knock on the door. Maltster instantly wakes up. He is quite sober
now and behaves exactly the way he did at the beginning of the play.
Clearly he has forgotten everything that went beforehand*

Maltster Come in.

The door opens with a creak and Vaněk enters with a sigh of relief

Vaněk That's better!

Maltster Ah, Mr Vaněk! Come on in.

*The door is closed. Vaněk's footsteps can be heard on the plain
wooden floor*

Sit down.

The chair scrapes the floorboards. Vaněk sits down

Have a lager.

Vaněk Sure.

Maltster pulls a bottle out of the crate, opens it and pours two glasses. He pushes one across the desk towards Vaněk

Maltster Here—
Vaněk Thanks. (*He at once gulps down his beer, smacking his lips*) How about the other half, then?

Maltster pours Vaněk another glass

Maltster Here you are, mate.
Vaněk (*gulping down the beer*) Ah!
Maltster (*after a pause*) Well, how's everything?
Vaněk Eh, screw it all! The lot!

CURTAIN

FURNITURE AND PROPERTY LIST

On stage: Desk. *On it:* papers, empty bottles, a bottle opener and two
                glasses
                Two creaky wooden chairs
                Crate of bottled beer

Off stage: Nil

Personal: Nil

LIGHTING PLOT

Property fittings required: nil

Interior. The same throughout

To open: Full general lighting

No cues

EFFECTS PLOT